# gospel-centered

# Marriage

*becoming the couple*
*God wants you to be*

Tim Chester

**the**good**book**
COMPANY

The Good Book Company
**Tel:** 866 244 2165
**Email:** admin@thegoodbook.com

**Websites:**
**N America:** www.thegoodbook.com
**UK:** www.thegoodbook.co.uk
**Australia:** www.thegoodbook.com.au
**New Zealand:** www.thegoodbook.co.nz

Unless otherwise indicated, Scripture quotations taken from the HOLY BIBLE, NEW
INTERNATIONAL VERSION. Copyright © 1973, 1978, 1984 by International Bible Society.
Used by permission of Hodder & Stoughton Publishers, A member of the Hachette Livre UK
Group. All rights reserved. "NIV" is a registered trademark of International Bible Society. UK
trademark number 1448790.

**Acknowledgments**
Chapters 1-2 and 11-14 are adapted from Tim Chester, *Captured By A Better Vision: Living
Porn Free*, IVP, 2010 and *Closing the Window: Steps to Living Porn Free*, InterVarsity, 2010.

ISBN (print): 9781908317582
ISBN (epub): 9781907377815
ISBN (kindle): 9781907377822

Cover design: Steve Devane
Printed in the USA

# Contents

# Introduction

The reign of Solomon was the golden age of Israel's history, a period of great learning, wisdom and literature. Some of this was inspired by God's Spirit and so became part of God's word: wisdom for life, meditations on suffering, songs of praise. One of these books is called Solomon's *Song of Songs*, a way of saying that this is *the best* of songs. How does this best of songs begin? "Let him kiss me with the kisses of his mouth – for your love is more delightful than wine" (Song 1 v 1-2). They are the words of a young woman asking for a kiss. The song is a celebration of romance, marriage, sex and kissing.

This book is about gospel-centered marriage. Most of what the Bible has to say about marriage does not come flagged up under a heading of "marriage". It's not just the famous "marriage passages" that shape a gospel-centered marriage, but the whole Bible-story of God's good creation, humanity's wicked rebellion and God's gracious redemption. To understand why marriages struggle—as they all do—we need to understand the nature of our sin. To make marriages work, we need to understand how to apply the truth about God and His salvation.

We'll discover, too, that perhaps the main reason why God created marriage and sexuality was to teach us the nature of His passionate commitment to His people. So marriage illustrates the gospel. The more we understand about the gospel, the more our marriages will be fit for purpose. And the more our marriages are fit for purpose, the better they will proclaim the gospel to people around us.

A couple of words of caution before we begin.

*First*, people often, unhelpfully, make their personal experience normative—the measure of everyone else's experience. This is especially true in marriage. So let's try to hear what God says in His word, rather than assume that our perspective is the rule.

And let's try to hear what God is saying *to us* in His word. We all have a tendency to apply Scripture to others before we apply it to ourselves. Again, this is especially true in marriage. So think about yourself first and foremost as you read, rather than about your spouse or other people you know.

*Second*, there are no perfect marriages. No perfect wives. No perfect husbands. Except Jesus Christ.

But there is an endless supply of grace. The church is the bride for whom Christ "gave himself up ... to make her holy, cleansing her by the washing with water through the word, and to present her to himself as a radiant church, without stain or wrinkle or any other blemish, but holy and blameless" (Ephesians 5 v 25-27). There's no need to hide or pretend. To a greater or lesser extent, you are a failure as a husband or wife. But the blood of Jesus covers and forgives that failure.

A few reflection questions are specific to those approaching marriage, but apart from that, I've written this book both for couples who have been married for many years and for people who are preparing to get married. What I've not included is material on raising children. For a gospel-centered approach to parenting, see the companion volume *Gospel-centered family*, available from The Good Book Company.

# Finding your way around

## Consider this

A scenario—often based on a real-life situation—which raises some kind of dilemma or frustration in marriage.

## Biblical background

A relevant Bible passage together with some questions to help you think it through.

## Read all about it

A discussion of the principle, both in terms of its theological underpinning and its contemporary application.

## Questions for reflection

Questions that can be used for group discussion or personal reflection.

## Ideas for action

Some ideas or an exercise to help people think through the application of the principle to their own situation.

*We have tried to make this book work:*

- whether it is read by an individual or used as the basis for group discussion.

- whether you want to work through it systematically or turn to particular topics as they arise.

# gospel-centered marriage

# 1 Marriage and the passion of God

**Principle**

Your marriage is an illustration of the relationship of Christ to His people.

## Consider this

Tom and Mary are about to have sex for the first time. It's their fourth date. They've been to see a movie and now Mary has invited Tom back for "coffee".

Across town, Jake and Sue are also about to have sex for the first time. It's their honeymoon night. The wedding was great—well, except for one family argument and one vomiting child. They're tired, but excited.

*What does each couple feel about having sex for the first time? What difference do Jake and Sue's wedding vows make to the way they feel about sex?*

Three weeks later Tom and Mary are arguing. Across town, so are Jake and Sue. Both arguments are heated: shouting, tears, silence.

*What does each couple feel about their argument? What difference do Jake and Sue's wedding vows make to the way they feel about conflict?*

## Biblical background

*Read Hosea chapters 1 – 3*

❓ How does Hosea's marriage point to God's relationship with His people?

❓ Identify some of the emotional language used to describe God's relationship with His people.

**Read all about it**

> *"Marriage is not a word. It's a sentence.*
> *A life sentence."*
> *"All men are born free, but some of them get married."*
> *"I never knew what happiness was until I got married and by*
> *then it was too late."*
> *"When a man holds a woman's hand before marriage, it is love;*
> *after marriage, it is self-defense."*
> *"Love is holding hands in the street; marriage is holding*
> *arguments in the street."*

Our culture doesn't always have a high view of marriage. The evidence suggests that married couples enjoy better sex than co-habiting couples, but you'd never guess that from movies and television. We have thousands of songs about falling in and out of love. Very few celebrate staying in love.

We all bring baggage to marriage. The baggage of our parents' marriage, past relationships, current tensions, cultural perspectives. All this can make it hard for us to grasp God's remarkable and beautiful vision of marriage. There's nothing new in this. When the disciples heard Jesus set out God's expectations for marriage, they said: "If this is the situation between a husband and wife, it is better not to marry" (Matthew 19 v 10).

## A picture of God's passionate love

The covenant of marriage is an echo of God's covenant relationship with His people. Throughout the Bible, God's relationship with His people is described as a marriage. "When I passed by again, I saw that you were old enough for love. So I wrapped my cloak around you to cover your nakedness and declared my marriage vows. I made a covenant with you, says the Sovereign LORD, and you became mine" (Ezekiel 16 v 8, NLT).

The unfaithfulness of God's people is described as adultery (Hosea 1 – 3). But God also promises to take His people back as His wife.

> *"But then I will win her back once again.*
> *I will lead her into the desert*
> *and speak tenderly to her there ...*
> *"When that day comes," says the LORD,*
> *"you will call me 'my husband'*
> *instead of 'my master' ...*
> *"I will make you my wife forever,*
> *showing you righteousness and justice,*
> *unfailing love and compassion.*
> *"I will be faithful to you and make you mine,*
> *and you will finally know me as the LORD"*
> **Hosea 2 v 14, 16, 19-20** *(NLT)*

> *Husbands, love your wives, just as Christ loved the church and gave himself up for her to make her holy, cleansing her by the washing with water through the word, and to present her to himself as a radiant church, without stain or wrinkle or any other blemish, but holy and blameless ... "For this reason a man will leave his father and mother and be united to his wife, and the two will become one flesh." This is a profound mystery—but I am talking about Christ and the church.* **Ephesians 5 v 25-27, 31-32**

In Ephesians 5, Paul quotes the words from Genesis 2 by which God first instituted marriage. But, says Paul, I'm actually talking about **Christ** and the **church**. Marriage was always intended to be a picture of Christ's relationship with His people. It's not just that God thought it was an appropriate illustration. God invented marriage, romance and sex to show us how He loves us!

- If you've experienced the joy of marriage, then you know something of the joy of companionship with God.
- If you've experienced the longing of singleness, then you know something of the need for God that we have.
- If you've experienced the pain of betrayal, then you know something of God's holy jealousy for the love of His people.
- If you've had any experience of passion, whether requited or unrequited, you know something of the passion of God for His people.

Whatever our experience, marriage and sexuality were given by God to show us the nature of His passionate love for His people.

### A picture of God's covenant love

Marriage is a covenant. That's not a word we often use. Our nearest equivalent is "contract", which reminds us that our marriage vows are solemn and legally binding. But "contract" makes it sound like a cold business deal. A covenant is a contract *with love*. The Bible has a special word for it: *hesed,* which means "covenant love" or "steadfast love". It's used to describe human faithfulness, but it also describes God's covenant love for His people—a love to which He has bound Himself through His word (Hebrews 6 v 13-20). Our faithfulness in marriage is modeled on God's faithfulness to us.

The great thing about marriage is that it is a combination of binding promises and loving relationship. There is love, but there is also a wedding ring to remind the lovers of their covenant promises. For those binding promises protect the loving relationship. The promises are its context, its framework, its protection. We're not called to keep *feeling* in love; we're called to keep *being* in love—by keeping our covenant promises.

This doesn't mean love is unimportant. Listen to the Song of Songs 8 v 6-7 (ESV):

> Set me as a seal upon your heart,
>   as a seal upon your arm,

> *for love is strong as death,*
> *  jealousy is fierce as the grave.*
> *Its flashes are flashes of fire,*
> *  the very flame of the* L*ord*.
> *Many waters cannot quench love,*
> *  neither can floods drown it.*
> *If a man offered for love all the wealth of his house,*
> *  he would be utterly despised.*

The Song of Songs may have been a celebration of, or even a polemic for, passionate, romantic love in the context of functional marriage—at least forced arranged marriages. In 8 v 11-12 the young woman asserts that, while literal vineyards can be hired out, her "vineyard" is for her to give and cannot be bought for money.

What this means is that love can sometimes be a *choice* rather than a *feeling*. More often the feeling of being "in love" *follows* the choice to love with steadfast covenant love. That's what happens in many, many arranged marriages. Similarly, I feel more in love than ever with my wife after over twenty years of marriage. It's because of all we've shared together—good and bad—and because of thousands of choices—large and small—that my wife has made to love me. Her committed covenant love fuels my feelings of being in love.

## Questions for reflection

- ❓ What do you love about your spouse?
- ❓ What do they do that gives you pleasure?
- ❓ What has your experience of marriage, singleness, love, romance or sex taught you about God's love for His people?

# 2 Marriage and the purposes of God

**Principle**

The purpose of your marriage is companionship and partnership in mission.

## Consider this

"What's wrong?" asked Brian. "I'm a great provider. Debbie wants for nothing. We have a beautiful home, great holidays, two lovely children, two cars, a dog. I'm a good husband. I've done everything I can for her. I'm home most evenings. I'm doing well at work. We have plenty of money. We go to church on Sunday. I'm attentive. We're like the model family! But we just seem to get on one another's nerves. Something's missing. There's no energy. No purpose."

Simon paused. There was much to admire in Brian. He was a good husband. Almost too good. Was that possible? Brian was right. There was something missing.

## Biblical background
*Read Genesis 1 v 26-28 and 2 v 18-24*

- ❓ What is the task given to humanity?
- ❓ What is God's solution for Adam's "alone-ness"?
- ❓ What does Eve provide for Adam?
- ❓ What does this tell us about marriage?
- ❓ Traditionally, people have suggested three different purposes for marriage: having children, protecting us from sexual temptation and providing for loneliness. After reading Genesis 1 and 2, do you think these are right?

**Read all about it**

A covenant of love describes the nature of marriage. But what is its purpose? What is marriage *for*?

Some Christians say marriage is for **procreation**. They stress the command to the first man and woman to "be fruitful and increase in number" (Genesis 1 v 28).

**True:** Marriage is the God-given context for children to grow up in. It offers stability, role models, a partnership of care. The command to "be fruitful and increase in number" means all marriages should be open to children.

**But:** If marriage is just about having babies, then childless marriages would be lesser marriages, and marriages would be redundant once children have left home. In fact the Song of Songs, the Bible's great celebration of married love, never mentions children! A marriage focused on children will struggle if the couple are childless or when the children leave home. And if their parents' marriage revolves around them, children will think they're the center of the world.

Some Christians say marriage is for **protection**. They emphasize 1 Corinthians 7 v 9: "It is better to marry than to burn with passion."

**True:** Marriage is the proper context for sexuality to find expression in intercourse. God forbids sex outside of marriage.

**But:** Marriage was given before humanity fell into sin, so it's not just a way of coping with our sinful desires. A marriage focused on sex will struggle because, if the goal of your marriage is sex, then sex is your true love and your spouse is just the means.

## *Companionship*

Some Christians say marriage is for **companionship**. And we see that this is the true purpose for marriage in Genesis 2 v 18: "The LORD God said, 'It is not good for the man to be alone. I will make a helper suitable for him.'" Marriage is for companionship ("It is not good for the man to be alone") and for service ("I will make a helper suitable for him").

God declared His creation very good (Genesis 1 v 31). *But there was one thing that was not good.* It was not good for man to be alone. God's response was to provide a wife for Adam. Marriage was God's idea. Despite the endless jokes about the inadequacies of women or men, God designed women as the "suitable" counterpart to men and *vice versa*. And God Himself was the first Father to give away a bride: "he brought her to the man" (Genesis 2 v 22).

In Song of Songs 8 v 10 (ESV) the woman says: "I was in his eyes as one who brings peace". (see the ESV footnote). She is the one who brings him *shalom*. The Hebrew word *shalom* means peace, but it means more than peace. It means rest and contentment, wholeness and completeness. She is the one who makes him whole, who completes him. In 6 v 13 she is his "Shulammite girl". There's no known place called Shulam so it probably means "his girl of *shalom*" or "his *shalom*-bringing girl". She gives him rest and makes him complete.

This doesn't mean I should approach marriage as a solution to *my* loneliness. Marriage doesn't primarily meet my *desire* to be loved (loneliness). It is one solution to my *need* to love and serve another (alone-ness). Our greatest need is to love God and to love others. Marriage provides "another" for us to love.

So companionship is not just about my emotional desires, but also about my need to give, to serve and to love. If they're not careful, single people can become self-indulgent over time, making decisions without reference to anyone else with only themselves to please. Marriage forces us to structure our lives around another.

A married person can't continue to live like a single person. But singleness is not to be considered as "second best". Because, as the story of redemption unfolds, the Bible also develops a vision for singleness with the creation of a new family, a freedom to serve in mission and a greater reward. See Mark 3 v 33-35; 1 Corinthians 7 v 7-8, 32-35; Isaiah 54 v 1-5; 56 v 1-5.

If your goal in marriage is to be loved (rather than to love), then you'll use your love as a means to get, or as a reward for, the love you crave. This can very quickly spiral downwards as each person withholds love to punish or control their spouse.

## Partnership

The woman is not only a *companion* for man's alone-ness, she is a *helper* for man's service. They are partners in the task God has given humanity. The task of filling the earth through having children clearly requires male and female, and marriage is the God-given context for conceiving and raising children.

But the task of humanity is more than procreation. The task is to reflect God's glory in His world as His image. It is to rule over the world, to take the world God has given and reflect His creativity in developing culture, science, knowledge, community and so on. With the story of sin and redemption the task takes a new turn. We become involved in the work of *re*creation. We proclaim the good news of a crucified King, who has paid the price of His people's rebellion; and a risen King, who commands our allegiance.

To some people it is given to serve God best as a single person (Matthew 19 v 12; 1 Corinthians 7 v 32-35), sometimes temporarily, sometimes throughout their life. But to many it is given to serve God in the partnership of marriage. If you're married, then your marriage is to be *a partnership of service*. That doesn't mean you always serve together. But it does mean you support one another in your service of God.

Marriages can so easily become introverted and indulgent. The couple spend much of their time with each other. Because marriage is a good thing, this is often justified with fine-sounding Christian language. But your marriage is not your own. It is a gift for service (just as singleness is a gift for service, 1 Corinthians 7 v 7).

Introverted marriages eventually shrivel—they become small marriages with small horizons. Your family is part of a bigger family of faith that demands your primary allegiance (Mark 3 v

31-35). It's great to spend time alone together, but recognize that you can bond just as well through serving together. So hold time alone lightly because *serving Christ* is the focus of your marriage.

Your marriage belongs to God. It is to be offered to Him and consecrated for His glory.

 **Questions for reflection**

Sometimes couples can serve together (offering hospitality in the home, co-leading a small group, sharing friendships). Sometimes they will serve separately (in the workplace, in gender-specific or specialist activities, when having young children means that one parent must baby-sit). When they serve separately, couples can still share their ministry by supporting one another in their respective service.

? What opportunities do you have to serve God together?

? What opportunities do you have to support one another's service of God?

When one spouse is not a Christian, then clearly you can't serve God in mission together (though it still may be possible to care for God's world together).

? How should a Christian serve God in their marriage when their spouse is not a believer? **See 1 Peter 3 v 1-2.**

**Ideas for action**

## For married couples

Spend some one-to-one time with your spouse, reflecting on the following questions:

- [?] If you took away children (or the possibility of children), what would be the state of your marriage?

- [?] If you took away sex, what would be the state of your marriage?

- [?] How much do you confide in one another? Does one of you feel that the other keeps part of themselves back or doesn't share what's in their heart?

- [?] When did you last have a date together? A night away without children?

- [?] Is your home open to serve others through hospitality?

- [?] Do you have friends in common?

- [?] Review the balance between time with just the two of you, time as a family and time together with other people.

## For couples approaching marriage

For each of the following, write your expectations and what you think are your partner's expectations. Then talk through your lists (preferably with an older Christian couple).

1. Your future plans and careers.
2. The balance of time together and time apart.
3. Your hopes for children and approach to parenting.
4. Responsibilities in the home.
5. Decision-making.
6. Conflict and conflict resolution.
7. Lifestyle and money.
8. Parents and in-laws.
9. Sex.
10. How you will serve God together and support one another's service.

# 3 Marriage and the kingdom of God

**Principle**

Your marriage is to demonstrate that it is good to live under God's reign.

 **Consider this**

Joan had been meeting up with her friend Christine to look at the Bible for some weeks now. As they caught up with news, they were chatting about married life.

"I know," said Joan. "My Bill can be a pain. When he comes in, he just moans about his boss and then asks when dinner's going to be ready. He never asks about my day. Then yesterday he said we can't afford to go on holiday this year. Well, that led to some shouting, I can tell you. But I'll get my way in the end. If sulking doesn't do it, I'll resort to the ultimate sanction in a wife's arsenal: no sex!"

Christine laughed. "Always works for me."

After some more light-hearted chat, they opened their Bibles. Together they read from Mark 1.

> *Jesus went into Galilee, proclaiming the good news of God.*
> *"The time has come," he said. "The kingdom of God is near.*
> *Repent and believe the good news!"*

"What's the kingdom of God?" asked Christine.

"It means God is going to reign over the world and that reign has begun with Jesus because Jesus is God's King. He can be Lord of our lives."

"He can be Lord of my life? That doesn't sound like good news! I don't want someone else being lord of my life. Especially not a man."

Joan didn't know what to say next. Christine was right. It didn't sound like good news at all.

**Biblical background**

*Read Ephesians 5 v 22-33*

- ❓ What does Paul tell wives to do?
- ❓ What does this mean in practice?
- ❓ What does Paul tell husbands to do?
- ❓ What does this mean in practice?

 **Read all about it**

Jesus began His ministry by proclaiming the good news (or "gospel") that the kingdom of God was near (Mark 1 v 14-15). God's kingdom was coming because God's King was coming. Good news. Gospel.

Except that the rule of God doesn't sound much like good news in our culture. We don't want someone else ruling over us. So how can the rule of God be good news?

It's a lie as old as humankind. It was the lie back in the Garden of Eden, when the serpent portrayed God as a tyrant holding Adam and Eve back. The serpent portrayed God's rule as oppressive and manipulative. But in reality, God's rule is a rule of blessing, freedom, love, life, justice and peace. It's good news. It's gospel.

But what's this got to do with marriage? The Bible says: "Wives should submit to their husbands in everything" (Ephesians 5 v 24). And immediately we think of patriarchal societies in which men have all the power. We think of inferiority and inequality. It makes us uncomfortable—and with good reason!

Because we have rejected God's rule, we not only get *God* wrong, we get *authority* wrong. We take over. And we rule—not like God, but like Satan's lie about God. We rule in a way that is self-serving and tyrannical. No wonder women resist that.

When humanity rejected God's authority, it radically altered the way marriages work. After our rebellion, God said to the first wife: "You will desire to control your husband, but he will rule over you" —or "dominate" you (Genesis 3 v 16, NLT).

> *The wife resists authority.*
> *The husband abuses authority.*

The Bible is the story of God saying: "My rule isn't like that". God sent His own Son, Jesus, to this world; and Jesus said He "did not come to be served, but to serve, and to give his life as a ransom for many" (Mark 10 v 45). Jesus our King died in our place on the cross. If you want to really know what God's rule is like, then look at the cross and see your King dying in your place to bring you freedom from your slavery to sin and self and death.

In Ephesians 5 Paul says marriage was designed to illustrate God's relationship with His people. There will be times when you say to your friends: "Jesus is Lord so turn from running your own life and trust in Jesus". And people will think: "Why is that good news? Why should I want to stop running my life and let God take charge?" And they should look at your marriage and say: "Ah, that's why! I can see it's good to live under authority like that. Maybe it really is good to live under God's authority."

## Submission and love

The Bible says: "Wives, submit to your husbands as to the Lord ... Husbands, love your wives, just as Christ loved the church" (Ephesians 5 v 22, 25).

Submission and love are very close. Both mutual love and mutual submission are commended within the wider body of Christ (5 v 2, 21). Clearly also, the wife is to love her husband and there is a sense in which it's appropriate for a husband to submit to his wife as one believer to another.

It's not difficult to see when this might operate. A wife might say to her husband: "My love, I hope you don't mind me mentioning it, but I don't think the way you spoke to Jack was appropriate". And a godly husband might say in those circumstances: "You're right. I was out of line. Thanks for pointing it out. I love the way you love me enough to challenge me. I'll give him a call to apologize."

## What's the difference?

But submission and love also have their differences, since in Ephesians 5 the relationship between husband and wife is compared to the relationship between Christ and the church. My relationship to Christ is not a mirror of His relationship with me. Christ does not submit to me!

Men and women are equal. But equality does not rule out having complementary roles or "headship"—one person being in charge. The place we see this clearly is in the doctrine of the Trinity. The persons of the Trinity are equal in terms of their being (their "God-ness" if you like). But the Son joyfully submits to the Father: He puts the will of the Father before His own (John 5 v 19; 8 v 28 etc.) This is the point Paul makes in 1 Corinthians 11 v 3. "Now I want you to realize that the head of every man is Christ, and the head of the woman is man, and the head of Christ is God." Or consider how we submit to political authorities or employers (1 Peter 2). We don't think it makes us less equal or less significant as people. But we do recognize different roles and different authority.

So what do submission and love mean in practice?

- The wife puts her husband's will before her own.
- The husband puts his wife's interests before his own.

This captures the similarities in their respective attitudes. But it also captures the differences. It gives the husband a lead role, but a lead role defined by the cross—one which seeks the good of the other rather than self-interest. It also captures how their respective roles correspond to the roles of the church towards Christ, and of Christ towards the church.

This doesn't mean (to anticipate the *"But what about...?"*

questions) that we must defend all the abuses of male headship over women. Quite the opposite!

The big issue here is what it means to exercise authority. Our problem is that we understand authority in the image of Satan's lie as *tyrannical*, rather than in the image of God's rule, which is *liberating*. Men believe the lie when they abuse authority; women believe the lie when they reject headship. Men abuse authority because they're self-interested; wives reject submission because they are self-willed.

## The way of the Spirit

When I look at Christian wives, I should see what it means to submit to Christ's authority—not begrudgingly, not with whining, but joyfully and freely. And when I look at Christian husbands, I should see what it means to exercise authority—not in a way that is self-serving, but loving and sacrificial. That's a high standard—for both sexes! And we might look at this ideal and think: "There's no way I can live up to that!"

In Ephesians, these words follow the exhortation to "be filled with the Spirit" (5 v 18), which is vitally important. If you are a Christian, God Himself is living in you, giving a new desire and a new power to live the right way. "I pray that out of his glorious riches he may strengthen you with power through his Spirit in your inner being, so that Christ may dwell in your hearts through faith" (3 v 16-17).

**Questions for reflection**

▪ What attitudes to the roles of husband and wife do you see among your friends, or in the wider culture of TV, films and magazines?

▪ How have these attitudes influenced you, both positively and negatively?

▪ Which marriages have influenced you most?

▪ What is it in other people's marriages you would like to copy?

▪ What things have you seen in other people's marriages that you would like to avoid?

▪ How is authority and submission exercised in the marriages you would like to emulate? How about in the marriages you would like to avoid?

# 4 Marriage and the submission of God's people

As the church submits to Christ, so wives put their husband's will before their own.

 **Consider this**

The conversation round the table was loud and raucous:

"Oh Pete and I never argue. It's simple. I make decisions about our home and holidays while Pete makes decisions about work and church."

"Our marriage is a partnership so we decide everything together."

"Well, we talk about big spending decisions together, but mostly he lets me get on with the money side of things because I'm so much better at figures than him."

"Colin thinks he's in charge, but I can always get him to do what I want. I just need to get all emotional and he'll cave in."

"Bruce calls all the shots in our marriage. Like I'd love to come to church with the rest of you, but Bruce would never let me."

"Well, often there can be a pretty heated discussion. Well, more of an argument I suppose! But in the end I usually agree we should do what Greg thinks best."

"I always do what Peter tells me... once I've told him what to say!"

The advise Jane received from her married friends left her more confused than ever.

*Whose example was she supposed to follow?*

## Biblical background

*Read 1 Peter 3 v 1-7*

❓ What does it mean for a wife to submit to her husband?

❓ What does it not mean?

❓ How is a husband to treat his wife?

## Read all about it

In our culture, where authority and submission are viewed with such suspicion, we need to spell out clearly what submission means and what it doesn't mean. 1 Peter 3 v 1-2 says: "Wives, in the same way be submissive to your husbands so that, if any of them do not believe the word, they may be won over without words by the behavior of their wives, when they see the purity and reverence of your lives." Notice what submission does *not* mean:

⬇ **Submission does not mean agreeing with everything your husband says,** for the wife of 1 Peter 3 believes Jesus is Lord whereas her husband does not.

⬇ **Submission does not mean never trying to change your husband,** for the wife of 1 Peter 3 is trying to convert him through her godly life.

⬇ **Submission does not mean a wife gets her spiritual strength from her husband,** for the wife of 1 Peter 3 cannot gain spiritual strength from her husband.

⬇ **Submission does not mean acting out of fear,** for the wife of 1 Peter 3 is told "do what is right without fear of what your husbands might do" (3 v 6, NLT).

What then is submission? Paul says: "Wives, submit to your husbands as to the Lord. For the husband is the head of the wife as Christ is the head of the church, his body, of which he is the Savior.

Now as the church submits to Christ, so also wives should submit to their husbands in everything" (Ephesians 5 v 22-24).

## Your husband's will before your will

Marriage brings a change of allegiance. When Paul wrote, the wife was usually living with her parents when she got married. Marriage meant she now had to put her husband before her parents.

More often today women have left home before they get married. They live, as it were, under their own authority, making decisions for themselves. But with marriage that changes. God is saying, in effect: "Wives, submit to your husbands instead of just submitting to yourselves." You have to think about your husband now. You're not free to do as you wish. This means respecting his God-given authority over you. That's how Paul sums it up: "The wife must respect her husband" (Ephesians 5 v 33).

You're to submit to your husband in a way that illustrates what it means to submit to Christ. That's the model for our submission. That means submitting without whining and without manipulating. Paul's joy in Christ keeps bursting out in the letter of Ephesians. Submitting to Christ is an act of joy. Wives must model the freedom of submission. We do not lose our freedom when we submit to the authority of God—we find it!

## Christ's will before your husband's will

Some people stress that the two commands are reciprocal or conditional on one another. So the wife is only bound to submit if the husband is exercising his authority with the sacrificial love that Christ models. Others stress submission "in everything" (v 24), saying that wives should submit even if their husband is abusive. Neither view really captures what the Bible actually says, which is that:

*You must submit even when your husband is not perfect.*

The alternative is a cycle of recrimination in which the wife gradually withdraws her submission and the husband gradually withdraws his love. The result is that the church's glad submission to Christ is not modeled. What *is* being modeled is the very worst kind of church—where love for Christ is cold.

*But neither is submission weak and passive.* It should be robust and reinforced with gospel conviction. We should challenge one another, speaking the truth in love (4 v 15). But we don't do this for our own sake. We do this for the sake of Christ and His glory, and for the sake of our spouses and their holiness.

### A higher allegiance

Wives should put their husband's will before their own, but that doesn't mean they should put his will *first*—**first place always belongs to Jesus.**

Both husband and wife have a higher allegiance and a higher purpose: to submit to Christ and to seek His glory. This means, for example, there will be times when a wife will challenge her husband or reject his will—in order to be obedient to Christ's will.

There is one important difference between submitting to a husband and submitting to Christ: your husband is not God. He will make mistakes. He will make bad judgments. And sometimes you will need to challenge him because your top allegiance is to the Lord. You're to speak the truth in love to him (Ephesians 4 v 15). So the wife puts her husband's will before her own—but not before Christ's will.

**Questions for reflection**

Reflect on a recent significant decision that you made together.

❓ How did you go about making the decision?

❓ How did the decision-making process reflect the wife's responsibility to put her husband's will before her own?

❓ How did the decision-making process reflect the husband's responsibility to put his wife's interests before his own?

❓ What would you do differently?

❓ Are there areas in your life together where the wife is more able or has specialist knowledge? For example, she may be good with figures or organizing or anticipating problems. How can the wife exercise submission while the husband respects his wife's superior abilities in these areas?

Genesis 2 v 24 says: "For this reason a man will leave his father and mother and be united to his wife, and they will become one flesh". When a man gets married, he leaves his parents and makes his wife his primary commitment. And when a woman gets married, she now submits to her husband before her parents. So we need to continue to honor our parents without being controlled by them.

❓ In this light, assess together your relationship with your in-laws.

# 5 Marriage and the loving authority of Christ

As Christ loves the church, husbands put their wife's interests before their own.

 **Consider this**

Family life revolves around **Darren**. He sees himself as the provider and protector. He's in charge. No one sits in his chair. He always has the remote control. He expects his dinner to be ready at six o'clock. He routinely takes the initiative in family life, usually to impose his will.

**Patrick** believes men and women are essentially the same. He and his wife share the household chores and make family decisions together. He hates macho posturing and wouldn't dream of imposing his will on anyone. He never takes the initiative because he doesn't want to appear pushy.

**Liam** is one of the lads. Up for a laugh. He likes his boy's toys and his nights out. He doesn't take life too seriously. He doesn't want the hassle of responsibility. He's married, but he still lives a single lifestyle.

**Chris** looked round the office. Darren, Patrick and Liam. Which of these men would he be like when he and Jane got married?

## Biblical background

*Read Mark 10 v 40-45*

- ❓ How do unbelievers exercise authority?
- ❓ How do unbelieving husbands exercise authority?
- ❓ How are Christians to exercise authority?
- ❓ How did Jesus exercise authority?

## Read all about it

Domineering Darren, Passive Patrick and Laddish Liam. Each represents a caricature of what our culture thinks it means to be a man. But what about Jesus? Husbands must love their wives "just as Christ loved the church" (Ephesians 2 v 25). What is His authority like? The answer is: *love*. And what does His love look like?

### It is in the shape of a cross

His rule is sacrificial, serving and selfless.

Every bride looks radiant on her wedding day. Her husband starts marriage full of good intentions to serve her selflessly.

The problem is she isn't always radiant. Some days she's grumpy or annoying or withdrawn. But Christ didn't love us *because* we were radiant; He loved us to *make* us radiant.

And Christ gave up everything for us (Philippians 2 v 6-11). He put our needs before His own. He put our relationship with God before His own (Mark 15 v 34, 38). That's the standard for husbands. You must give up everything for your wife; put *her* relationship with God before your own; put *her* needs before your needs.

Christ loves us unconditionally, but He loves us with an agenda. He doesn't love us *because* we are radiant; he loves us to *make* us radiant.

And a husband is to love his wife unconditionally, not just when she's looking great or treating him well. But husbands should have an agenda, and that agenda is the same as Christ's agenda: to make her holy and blameless, to help her grow as a Christian.

To help her become more like Jesus.

There are no exceptions. You can't say: "I love my wife sacrificially, but today... today I'm tired, I'm not feeling well, I've got a lot on". That's why Paul goes on to say: "Husbands ought to love their wives as they love their own bodies". It's so concrete. You're tired. Your want to put your feet up. You want to relax in front of the TV. That's how you love your body. And that's how you're to love your wife. So you say: "No, darling, you sit down and I'll cook the dinner".

That's the test: care for her as you care for yourself. Most of us are very good at loving ourselves; we must love our wives with exactly the same passion.

This doesn't mean giving in passively to her wishes. I'm not being a servant leader in our marriage if I say: *"Whatever!"*

This is how Saturdays all too often work in our household. I love to putter around. Meanwhile my wife tries to initiate some family activity. I give in. Often reluctantly. Because I want to serve my wife. But, of course, my wife senses (correctly) that my heart's not in it. I've put her interests before my own, but only in a formal, passive sense.

*So what should I do?*

## I should take the lead

That doesn't mean deciding what I want to do and then dragging the family along reluctantly. That would be to lord it over my family, not serve them. Instead, it means coming up with a plan that I know will please my wife. Perhaps surprising her. It doesn't have to be anything elaborate or extravagant. Just a proactive plan that will bless her.

### Family decisions

The same principle can apply to family decision-making. Loving your wife doesn't mean lording it over her. But neither does it mean "just doing what she wants". It means actively putting her interests before your own. That means you'll need to study your wife to understand the things that are really in her interests.

So you're *not* being a good husband when you simply pursue your own interests, nor when you passively give in to your wife's wishes. You're being a good husband when you actively pursue the things that will help your wife blossom and grow. But there's a big difference between that, and just doing what she likes. At times you'll need to put your wife's holiness before her happiness.

A godly man takes the initiative. He takes responsibility in the home, in the church, and in the community. He takes the initiative to put out the chairs, to pray in the prayer meeting, to welcome new people, to resolve conflict, to volunteer in the neighborhood, or to check on elderly neighbors. And in marriage, too, the husband has *the responsibility to take the initiative*. That doesn't mean, of course, that the wife *can't* take the initiative. A husband ought to thank his wife when she takes the initiative, but he should feel it as something of a rebuke when she has to take the initiative in areas that should be his responsibility like:

- resolving conflict
- ensuring decisions are made in a godly way
- discipling and teaching children

That doesn't mean he does it all, but he can't abdicate responsibility to his wife.

**Questions for reflection**

What will it mean for "Adam" to sacrificially love "Eve" and for "Eve" to submit to "Adam" when...

**?** they allocate household chores?

**?** they disagree over holiday plans?

**?** Eve is anxious about money?.

**?** they're both tired and the housework needs doing?

**?** Eve wants to talk and Adam wants to watch the game?

**?** Adam hasn't done something Eve asked him to do, and so Eve feels he's neglectful, while Adam feels she's nagging him?

**Ideas for action**

## For husbands

Set aside some time each week to think about what you can do for your wife.

- ❓ How is her walk with God?

- ❓ How is her relationship with you?

- ❓ With what is she struggling?

- ❓ What encouragement does she need to receive?

- ❓ What gospel truth does she need to hear?

- ❓ What could you do to bless her?

- ❓ What could you do to express your affection for her?

You could make this part of your routine prayer time (along with time reflecting on how you could take the initiative to serve God in the home, the workplace and the neighborhood). Or you could use the journey home from work to prepare yourself to serve your wife.

# gospel-centered relationships

# 6 Grace

## Principle

Grace means we can always begin again.

## Consider this

"Can I talk to you about something?" Carl asked.

We've been talking for the last hour, thought Pete, but he knew what Carl meant: something personal. "Sure, go ahead."

"Well, Clare and I are getting married next month, as you know. And, well, she became a Christian three years ago and before that she had other sexual partners."

"Yes?"

"Well, I'm not sure what to do with that. Is it going to be a problem?"

"Maybe," said Pete. "It depends."

"It depends? On what?"

## Biblical background

*Read Titus 3 v 3-8*

?  How does the description of verse 3 affect our relationships with the opposite sex?

?  Verse 3 describes how things were "at one time" in the past. How does Paul describe Christians in the present?

?  What has happened to make this change?

?  What might "the washing of rebirth and renewal by the Holy Spirit" mean for sexual sins?

### Read all about it

On her wedding day the bride walks down the aisle looking radiant, as brides are wont to do. The groom is groomed, smiling, nervous, and relieved to see his bride approach. They hold hands fondly, look lovingly at each other as they make their vows, while various aunts wipe tears from their eyes. Everything is magical. And then the next morning you wake up to find a sinner in bed with you.

It's not enough to work at marriage. That's legalism. You will fail. Your spouse will fail. Not only will it lead to failure, but if you think you can make your marriage work through your effort, then the failure will be devastating. Where do you go next? If you work really hard and hard work doesn't work, what's Plan B? So here are some key truths.

## Marriage is a scary union of two sinners

There are two basic problems in every marriage: one is the husband and the other is the wife. We're all self-obsessed, self-centered, sinful human beings who want the world to revolve around us. Marriage throws two such individuals into close proximity.

So get used to it. Don't expect perfection. Don't expect it of yourself. And don't expect it of your partner. Aim for it. Work hard for it. But also be ready for failure, for misunderstanding, for conflict, for tension, for sin. Be ready with the grace of God.

> *Do you not know that the wicked will not inherit the kingdom of God? Do not be deceived: Neither the sexually immoral nor idolaters nor adulterers nor male prostitutes nor homosexual offenders nor thieves nor the greedy nor drunkards nor slanderers nor swindlers will inherit the kingdom of God. And that is what some of you were. But you were washed, you were sanctified, you were justified in the name of the Lord Jesus Christ and by the Spirit of our God.*
>
> **1 Corinthians 6 v 9-11**

There's some pretty X-rated stuff here. But Paul says: "You were washed ... sanctified ... justified". It's cleaned away. You're declared holy. You're declared right in God's sight. You don't need to carry your baggage. You're not spoiled goods. You're goods that have been washed and made new.

## Grace for future change

*For the grace of God that brings salvation has appeared to all men. It teaches us to say "No" to ungodliness and worldly passions, and to live self-controlled, upright and godly lives in this present age, while we wait for the blessed hope—the glorious appearing of our great God and Savior, Jesus Christ, who gave himself for us to redeem us from all wickedness and to purify for himself a people that are his very own, eager to do what is good.* **Titus 2 v 11-14**

The gospel addresses our passions, including our sexual passions. It offers hope for change. Jesus is setting us free from wickedness. He's purifying for Himself a people as His very own. Grace is teaching us self-control. Grace is setting us free. Grace is purifying us. This process takes a lifetime, but it is a process of real change.

This is true of you. It's also true of your spouse.

It can often seem as if the past continues to haunt both parties. Patterns of behavior in relationships or in sex may still affect the way you react to each other. Previous empty relationships may have taught you to objectify your partner in sex (to view them as an object through which you can get sexual satisfaction). Past hurts may have taught you to mistrust others. Former abuse may have given you a negative view of sex. You may fear comparison with previous partners.

But we are new creations in Christ (2 Corinthians 5 v 17).

That means that your past need not define you, nor determine your future. It means that your spouse's past need not define them, nor determine your future together. If you are in Christ, the person you are now is not the person you once were. The person they are now is not the person they once were. We are washed, sanctified, justified.

The past teaches us to behave in certain ways—sometimes ungodly ways. But the grace of God teaches us to say "No" to ungodliness. The gospel teaches us to see the world—including sex and marriage—in a right perspective.

The past may be tough for you to cope with. But through the gospel we can cope and change and flourish.

## Grace for present failings

You had better learn to ask for forgiveness and to offer forgiveness. Otherwise your marriage will be in trouble because marriage is a scary union of two sinners. You will let each other down. You will forget. You will get angry. You will annoy. You will break promises. So be quick to forgive.

"Do not let the sun go down while you are still angry, and do not give the devil a foothold" (Ephesians 4 v 26-27). Sort things out within the day. If you don't, then the devil will get a foothold in your marriage. That unfinished business won't disappear. It will fester away. The devil will start to corrode your relationship.

**Questions for reflection**

Lord Melbourne apparently advised the young Queen Victoria: "In marriage, disagreements are not nearly as dangerous as secrets. Secrets breed mistrust."

❓ Do you have secrets from one another? Are there areas that are "off limits", that you can't talk about together?

**Ideas for action**

- No one ever decided one day to look for an affair. It's normally a gradual process that creeps up on you.
- Don't allow any distance to grow between you and your spouse.
- You're not responsible for being attracted to someone, but you are responsible for lingering looks and lingering thoughts.
- Don't indulge in "innocent" flirting.
- Be wary of deep conversations alone with a member of the opposite sex.
- Don't have secrets.
- Don't do anything you wouldn't tell your spouse about. Above all, make the choice to love your spouse and keep your covenant promises.

## For those approaching marriage

- Talk to your future spouse about past relationships.
- Tell them about any past sexual activity (including pornography) without going into too much detail. Focus on experiences that might affect your future together.
- Past experiences can shape our attitudes, expectations and behavior. But they don't have to.

# 7 Love

## Principle

Daily thoughtfulness matters more than grand gestures.

## Consider this

"It's beautiful," Aiesha thought. She was holding the necklace Dwayne had just given her and he was looking at her with a "tell-me-how-delighted-you-are" look on his face.

She was sitting on the sofa surrounded by children's toys. Ruby was on her lap, Leo hanging round her legs. Yesterday's dishes were still in the sink. Her bedroom smelled of disinfectant. She smelled of baby milk.

"It's beautiful," she said. "But when am I going to wear it?"

Dwayne's face sank. "I just wanted you to know that I love you," he said in a self-pitying voice.

Aiesha might have protested, but she was too tired.

## Biblical background
*Read John 13 v 1-17*

- What three things does John say Jesus knew as He washed the feet of His disciples (verses 1, 3, 11)?
- How do they undermine some of our common excuses for not sacrificially serving one another?
- How does Jesus apply His actions to us in verses 12-17?

**Read all about it**

### Men are from Mars, women are from Venus

Men and women are very different and we need to understand those differences if our marriages are going to work. That's the message of many popular books on relationships like John Gray's famous book, *Men are from Mars, Women are from Venus*.

And there's a lot in this claim.

Eve's had a bad day in the office. When she gets home, she tells Adam all about it: her unreasonable boss; her good-for-nothing colleague; the ridiculous new directive; the stupid deadline for a new report she has to write. Adam responds by suggesting some solutions.

"Why don't you talk to your boss's boss?"

"Why don't you cut and paste content from the report you wrote last week?"

Adam thinks he's being helpful. Eve came to him with a problem and he's suggested some solutions. "Oh, it's no good talking to you," Eve exclaims, locking herself in the bathroom and running a hot bath. "He thinks I'm stupid," she says to herself. "Like those ideas had never occurred to me! All I wanted was some sympathy."

Women want empathy. Men offer solutions. My wife had to teach me this. "Just stroke me and say: 'Poor Helen'. That's all I want."

Women typically use communication to establish connection and intimacy while men often use it to establish independence and status. This means women are inclined to do what they're asked while men initially resist to preserve their independence. So women repeat a request, thinking it will make it even more likely to happen. But men continue to ignore them, even more determined to resist. The result: nagging. It's also why men would rather remain lost than ask a stranger for help, or why they get their wives to ask.

So there is some truth in this view of male and female differences. But there are two big problems.

**First**, they're generalizations. They may be generally true, but not always. Don't treat your spouse as some kind of generic man or woman. *Study them!*

Work out how they work. What pleases them? What annoys them? How do they communicate love? How do they communicate frustration?

## Love is from the heart

**Second**, this approach misses the underlying issue in conflict and misunderstanding. *Men may be from Mars and women may be from Venus, but love is from the heart.* Our problem is not a lack of education about the other sex. *Our fundamental problem is our sinful hearts.* The Bible says our behavior comes from our hearts. It's not determined by our gender, but by our hearts. Gender differences (whether from nature or nurture) may shape our behavior, but the ultimate source of hurtful behavior and loving behavior is our heart.

The subtitle of John Gray's book, *How to Get What You Want In Your Relationships*, is very revealing. Learning how men or women think will not solve your marriage problems if your intention is just *to get what you want from your relationship*. The main reason I hurt my wife is not because I'm from Mars and she's from Venus. I hurt my wife because I have a sinful, selfish heart.

## Thoughtful love

It's very common for people (usually husbands) to be willing to make sacrifices for their wives, but never to take the trouble to anticipate what their wives want. But thoughtfulness is just as much an act of love as sacrifice. Indeed it is sacrificing one's own preoccupations, denying yourself and thinking about the other person. Love is looking at things from the other person's perspective.

Most wives don't want diamond rings and flowers every day. They want thoughtfulness, consideration, anticipation. That means things like putting dirty clothes in the basket, or wiping the kitchen surfaces after you've washed up, or checking with her before you say "Yes", or noticing what she's wearing. It means doing household chores and disciplining children without waiting to be asked. It means gifts whose value is not in what they cost, but the thoughtfulness that went into them ("I saw this and thought of you" rather than "I thought I ought to"). It means anticipation. Being one step ahead of your spouse's desires. Acting before being asked.

The good news is that *love is not complicated*. I don't need a degree in gender studies to love my spouse. *But love is also hard work*. The flip-side of love is self-denial. Love is putting someone else before myself: their interests, their wishes, their needs, their comfort. The fact that you desire your spouse and feel warm thoughts about them does not mean you love them. Nor is it any good loving someone in some abstract sense.

Love is washing dishes, cooking the dinner, putting the garbage out, not highlighting their faults, not worrying if they put things away in the wrong place, not buying the gadgets or clothes you want, but thinking about their feelings, listening to their point of view, asking about their day. And love covers over a multitude of sins. It's not that love discounts or dismisses sin. But it forbears and forgives. Love chooses to see annoying habits as charming foibles.

## The way of blessing

Putting someone else's will before your own or someone else's interests before your own doesn't sound like much fun. But this is the way of blessing. "Now that you know these things," says Jesus, "you will be blessed if you do them" (John 13 v 17).

In marriage we learn that we find our lives by giving up our lives. I give away the freedoms of a single man, but receive in return the greater joys of covenant love. I find the restrictions of marriage in fact enable me to be free—to be the person I was meant to be.

One of the refrains of the Song of Songs is: "My lover is mine, and I am his" (2 v 16; 6 v 3). It's the language of ownership and possession. In marriage you give yourself away and belong to another. But it is *mutual possession* and *mutual belonging*. In marriage I learn to enjoy belonging to another. The young woman of the Song delights that her lover claims her as his own. There's no striving for independence or autonomy, just a glad acceptance of mutual possession.

And so through marriage we learn what a delight it can be to say: "My Jesus is mine and I am His. He is Lord and He is *my* Lord. I belong to Him." We rejoice to hear God say again and again throughout the Bible story: "I will be your God and you will be my people".

I discover through marriage how serving someone else brings me pleasure. It's so tragic when couples are trying to get the most from each other. They may never have a full-blown argument, but there is this constant competition going on. Or responsibilities have to be negotiated. Or one party serves the other out of fear. Or getting the other to help is more trouble than it's worth.

Marriage and sex teach us that love is its own reward; that joy is found in service; that it is more blessed to give than to receive; that you gain your life by giving up your life.

 **Questions for reflection**

- ❓ How are you different from each other?
- ❓ How do you adapt to one another's differences?
- ❓ How would you like your spouse to adapt to you?
- ❓ What does your spouse do that you think is thoughtless?
- ❓ What does your spouse do that you think is thoughtful?

## Ideas for action

- **Study your spouse.** How do they like you to communicate? What form of communication speaks most to them?

- **Have some set times for each other.** My wife and I normally have a cup of tea together when she gets in from work and a prayer together last thing at night. We hold them with a light hand and as often as not we miss one because of meetings or late nights. But it still adds up to several times a week. They're the high points of my day. As things happen during the day, I often think about relating them to my wife. I end up with a list of things I want to tell her when she gets in from work.

- **Be a good listener:** Without interrupting, without presuming you understand, without defending your actions, without rationalizing their feelings. Good listening is not a technique you learn. It's the product of a loving heart. We listen well when we're genuinely interested in people and what they have to say.

- **Be interested in each other's interests.** My wife has learned to enjoy cricket and I've learned to do crosswords. You don't have to do everything together. It can be healthy to have separate hobbies. But take an interest. If your husband likes football, then follow his team even if you don't go to the game with him. If your wife joins a book club, then ask about what they're reading even if you don't read it yourself.

# **8** Conflict

**Principle**

Conflict begins when my selfish desires are denied by my spouse.

 **Consider this**

"She's always late," Dave said to Pete. "Always. Last night we didn't leave until eight o'clock. I was ready at 7.30."

"But we were only five minutes late," said Paula. "What's the big deal?"

"We said we'd be there at half past. You know I don't like to feel rushed. I want to feel everything's under control. Besides, I don't like to keep people waiting."

"You care too much about what people think."

"I care too much? What about you? I wasn't the one who took an hour to get ready. You're the one who wanted to impress people."

Pete wondered what he should say as his friends argued.

 **Biblical background**

*Read James 3 v 13-18*

? What is the result of envy and selfish ambition?

? What is the result of humility?

*Read James 4 v 1-6*

? What is the cause of conflict?

**Read all about it**

"I did it because he…" "I said it because she…"

I wonder if you've ever said anything like that. You attribute your behavior to the actions of your spouse. "It was her fault." "He started it." "She winds me up." "He never does anything to help." "You'd do the same." "The woman you put here with me—she gave me some fruit from the tree, and I ate it" (Genesis 3 v 12).

When there are problems in our marriage, we blame our spouse. My behavior was a reasonable and unavoidable response to her unreasonable and avoidable behavior.

## Heart problem

But, as we've seen, the source of all human behavior and emotions is the heart. The "heart" in the Bible refers to the inner person. It's not just my emotions—as it is in western culture, where we think with our heads and feel with our hearts. In the Bible the heart represents our thinking *and* desires. All our actions flow from the heart (Mark 7 v 20-23; Luke 6 v 43-45; Romans 1 v 21-25; Ephesians 4 v 17-24; James 4 v 1-10.) Circumstances, upbringing, hormones and our personal history all play a part in shaping our behavior, but the root problem is the sinful desires of the heart.

So we can never say: "The woman you put here with me—she gave me some fruit from the tree, and I ate it" (Genesis 3 v 12). Or: "The husband you gave me started it". "When tempted, no one should say, 'God is tempting me." For God cannot be tempted by evil, nor does he tempt anyone; but each one is tempted when, by his own evil desire, he is dragged away and enticed" (James 1 v 13-14). The pressures of marriage or the behavior of your partner may create the circumstances in which your idolatrous desires are expressed. They may be the trigger. *But they are never the cause. Our actions always come from the thoughts and desires of our hearts.*

A sinful desire is not just a desire for a bad thing. It can also be a desire for a good thing which has become bigger than God. To want to be respected by your wife or to want affection for your husband, for example, is to desire a good thing. But if my spouse makes me bitter, then my desire for respect or affection has grown too big— bigger than my desire for God—so that I can't be content with God's sovereignty over my life.

If couples do not address the idolatries in their marriage, then it's tragically possible to create a merely functional marriage—a marriage in which personal disclosure and intimacy are missing.

What are some of the idols at work within marriage? The desire for love, appreciation, thoughtfulness, understanding, justice, my own way, pleasure, sex, success, fun, security, comfort, peace, adoration, or respect. Most of these are good things. It's normal to *want* them. But when these desires matter more to us than God, or when we start talking about them as things we *need*, then they have become what the Bible calls "sinful desires of the heart".

### Marriage as an idol

And marriage itself can become an idol. People can crave marriage for what they can get out of it: not being left on the shelf, not being a nobody, having significance, enjoying intimacy. We need to view marriage as a good gift from God, but not worship it. Or perhaps we want to be seen to have the perfect marriage so others hold us in high regard. The result is we can't be honest about marital problems as they arise.

Your partner can become an idol. Your worth, significance or identity becomes dependent on their acceptance and approval. The response of our partner becomes more important than obedience to God. We crave their approval or fear their rejection because we're desperate for them to affirm (= worship) us.

If we make marriage or our spouse an idol, then we're not free to love them as we should. When we show them kindness, it's so they'll reward us with their affirmation, love, respect or intimacy. We love them for what we get in return. And that's not true love. The answer is to turn back constantly and repeatedly to God.

- If there are problems in my marriage because I feel the need to be in control, then hope is found in trusting God: God is great and I can trust His control.
- If there are problems in my marriage because I feel the need for my spouse's approval or want other people to admire my marriage, then hope is found in trusting God. Because God is glorious and His approval is what matters and His approval is what I already have in Christ.
- If there are problems in my marriage because I feel the need for intimacy or sex or fun, then hope is found in trusting God. Because God is good and He is the source of true joy.
- If there are problems in my marriage because I feel the need for affirmation or approval or admiration, then hope is found in trusting God. Because God is gracious and I can find identity in Christ.

A failure to believe one of these four liberating truths about God underlies nearly all our sinful behavior, marital conflict and negative emotions:

1. **God is great**—*so we don't have to be in control*
2. **God is glorious**—*so we don't have to fear others*
3. **God is good**—*so we don't have to look elsewhere*
4. **God is gracious**—*so we don't have to prove ourselves*

You can use these truths as a diagnostic tool to help identify what lies behind your sinful behavior, marital conflict or negative emotions.

They'll also help you speak the good news of the gospel to your spouse when they're struggling. "You shouldn't think that way" or "You shouldn't have done that" are not always helpful. It might be right, but it doesn't offer much hope. It's not gospel. But we can say: "You don't have to do that because Jesus offers so much more. He is great and glorious and good and gracious." And that's good news.

## Questions for reflection

? What might happen to your marriage if you stop trusting that:
1. God is great?
2. God is glorious?
3. God is good?
4. God is gracious?

*Can you see any signs of this happening?*

? How could you remind yourself of the truth you need to embrace so it touches your heart and imagination?

? How could you remind your spouse of the truth they need to embrace so it touches their heart and imagination?

# 9 Reconciliation

## Principle

Reconciliation begins when my selfish desires are denied by me.

 **Consider this**

"Can I say something?" Pete said.

Dave and Paula stopped arguing and turned to him, slightly surprised, as if they'd forgotten he was in the room. "Sure," said Dave. "Maybe you can talk some sense into her."

"Dave, why is being in control so important to you?"

"What do you mean?"

"Well, here you are arguing with the person you love most about being a few minutes late. Why is it such a big deal?"

"I like to leave plenty of time to get places."

"Nothing wrong with that. But why does it matter so much to you? Why is it making you so angry?"

"I like to be in control."

"But you're not in control, are you? Not really. But that's okay because God's in control. He's your Father looking after you. He won't let anything happen to you that's not part of His plan."

"I knew it was your fault," said Paula.

"And Paula," began Pete. "What about you?"

## Biblical background

*Read James 4 v 1-12*

❓ What is the cause of conflict? (See chapter 8.)

❓ What is the solution to conflict?

❓ What promises does God make in this passage?

## Read all about it

James 4 v 1 reveals the underlying causes of anger:

> *What causes fights and quarrels among you? Don't they come from your desires that battle within you?*

The root of conflict in marriage is the idolatrous desires of our hearts. When those desires are thwarted or threatened, we react. We may react with fighting or quarrels. We may react with anger, sulking, bitterness, resentment or complaining. All these responses are responses to thwarted or threatened desires. James says conflict comes from "your desires that battle within you".

When you have an argument with your spouse or when their behavior annoys you or when you feel resentful, try to discern those underlying idolatrous desires. One of the great things about marriage is that God throws a fellow sinner into close proximity to us so that they walk all over our idols. So marriage is a God-given means of revealing and addressing our idolatrous desires.

I have a desire for order. That's a good desire. It makes our family run well. But that desire can be idolatrous. Sometimes my wife puts things away in the wrong place. It's a small thing. But it annoys me. I get frustrated. That frustration is the sign that something is wrong. The bad fruit in my behavior is a sign of a bad root in my heart

(Luke 6 v 43-45). It might mean that what I *really want* is for life to be ordered *my way!* I want it to be all about me. And so when I don't get my way, then I get annoyed. So I need to learn again that God is the one that matters. And God is the one who is sovereign.

The following questions may help you dig underneath your behavior to discover the idols lurking deep within.

## 1. When do you respond badly to your spouse?

What triggers your response? Can you spot any patterns? You may consider one particular incident or a pattern of behavior. Identifying the points at which you get angry or bitter or resentful enables you to think about what you want in that situation.

## 2. How do you respond badly?

People express themselves in many different ways: some shout and stamp their feet; some come out with snide or sarcastic remarks; some bottle it up and then explode; some withdraw or go for the silent treatment. Some people may not see their reactions as sinful because they only associate sinful responses with rage. You may see yourself as a calm person because you don't shout and scream. But your inner attitude exhibits itself in the comments you make or your indifference to others.

## 3. What happens when you act badly?

Wisdom is revealed in a good life and deeds done in humility (James 3 v 13). It is "peace-loving, considerate, submissive, full of mercy and good fruit, impartial and sincere" (3 v 17). Envy and self-ambition, in contrast, produce "disorder and every evil practice" (3 v 16). Retell the story or stories of your conflict. Explore the results of your behavior or response. What harmful fruit are your actions producing in your life and your marriage?

## 4. Why do you act badly?

Our behavior is caused by "desires within" (James 4 v 1-4). We usually explain our behavior by pointing to our circumstances. ("I was provoked." "She pushed my buttons." "He was so unfair.") We need to recognize that we choose how to respond to those circumstances. We're not passive. Our behavior is not inevitable. It's caused by our idolatrous desires.

One of the ironies of conflict situations is that we blame the other party for *their* actions and we blame the other party for *our* actions as well!

"They're angry because they're in the wrong and I'm angry because they're in the wrong."

Our sinful instinct is to judge the other party and not ourselves. But James says, in effect: *Don't play God. Don't make yourself the judge* (James 4 v 11-12; see also Matthew 7 v 1-5). Even if the other person was worse than us, our responsibility is to repent of playing God.

Ask yourself: "What am I thinking?" and "What do I really want?" to identify your failure to trust God as you should and the idolatrous desires that control your heart. What makes me want to wage war (4 v 1-2) when Christ's rule should make me want to make peace (3 v 17-18)?

We act badly because we're not getting something that we want. This desire has won the battle for control of our hearts (4 v 1), leading to spiritual adultery (4 v 4).

### Right response 1: Ask God to show you the idolatrous desires that cause your behavior

James invites us to pray for wisdom (1 v 5). Biblical wisdom is about connecting biblical truth with everyday life. In the case of marital conflict, it means connecting our behavior with our idolatrous desires. Earthly wisdom means covering up jealousy and selfish ambition with boasting and lying (3 v 14). The result is disorder and evil of every kind. The wisdom that comes from heaven means seeing the world the way God does (3 v 13). The result is a harvest of righteousness (3 v 17-18). So pray for wisdom so that you and your spouse can understand the causes of your behavior.

### Right response 2: Humble yourself before God

"God opposes the proud but gives grace to the humble" (4 v 6-7). The desires within that cause conflict are all about me: jealousy, pride and selfishness (3 v 14-16). Somewhere in the middle of my behavior is the phrase: "I want…"

The solution is to humble ourselves before God. We need to stop exalting ourselves, pursuing our wants and trying to take control. Instead we must say: "I want what God wants and I'm happy that God is in control". In conflict we look down on others. We need to get lower. It's difficult to be angry when your cry is: "God, have mercy on me, a sinner" (Luke 18 v 13). When we come in humility to God, He gives us grace to change (4 v 6).

### Right response 3: Repent of your desires and behavior

All the time you blame other people or your circumstances, what happens to your sinful behavior? Nothing. It goes on seething, festering, harming and spoiling. But repentance sets us free. When we humble ourselves before God, He promises to lift us up (4 v 10). When we repent of our idolatrous desires, the provocations may still be there, but the sinful behavior and its destructive fruit are gone.

**Questions for reflection**

Reflect on a recent occasion when there was conflict in your marriage or you were resentful or angry with your spouse. Or reflect on a pattern of problem behavior. Use the framework above to identify the heart desires that caused your behavior and to identify the appropriate response.

1. When did you respond badly to your spouse?
2. How did you respond badly?
3. What happened when you acted badly?
4. Why did you act badly?

**Right response 1:** Ask God to show you the idolatrous desires that cause your behavior

**Right response 2:** Humble yourself before God

**Right response 3:** Repent of your desires and behavior

# 10 Forgiveness

Trust must be earned and forgiveness must be given.

 **Consider this**

Two years into their marriage Sue walked into Lloyd's study. She could tell something was wrong straight away. He stood up quickly, nudging the laptop away from her as his face reddened. She pushed past him and turned the laptop round. What she saw shocked her.

Porn.

"How long?" she demanded. "For a while." "How often?" "Occasionally." She turned away and walked out, tears beginning to well up in her eyes.

A couple of days later she sat with her friend, Emily. "It turns out that 'for a while' means 'from the beginning', and 'occasionally' means 'every week'! What am I going to do?"

 **Biblical background**

*Read Matthew 18 v 21-35*

🔲 How should we treat people who sin against us?

🔲 Why should we forgive others?

🔲 What is the limit of our forgiveness?

🔲 What about people who continue to sin against us?

**Read all about it**

Your husband buys a new gadget without asking you. Your wife announces that you're spending Christmas with her family without any consultation. Your husband breaks your favorite vase. Your wife says she's too tired to have sex. What happens next?

## It's not about you

When an argument occurs, I typically:
- defend myself
- put my perspective as the "real" one
- highlight the wrong done to me
- describe my hurt or embarrassment or disappointment

I'm at the center of the picture. What matters is that I'm vindicated or recompensed.

But it's not about you. Your life is not about you. Your marriage is not about you. You died when you came to Christ. You now live for Him. Your concern is God's glory. Your vindication is not what matters most.

From that perspective you may be able to see your own guilt.

Even if you're the injured party, you recognize that God is the more injured party. David said to God, when he had committed adultery with Bathsheba and murdered her husband, Uriah: "Against you, you only, have I sinned and done what is evil in your sight, so that you are proved right when you speak and justified when you judge" (Psalm 51 v 4). The central issue was *David and God*—not David and Bathsheba or David and Uriah.

So even when you're the injured party, the biggest issue is reconciliation between your spouse and your God. Your role is to disciple him or her to repentance and point them to grace.

## Look to the cross

The key is to look to the cross. At the cross we see our own sin. When we get the chance to kill our Creator, we do so. So the cross prevents any sense of self-righteousness. Even if I've been innocent in this issue, I'm not innocent. I'm not more innocent. I am only ever a rebel saved by grace.

The cross also means *you can't demand payment or recompense.* It's very tempting to punish your spouse for their actions—to be cold towards them, or be short with them. Snap at them. Withhold affection. Act selfishly.

But you're punishing them for an offense that's already been punished. If they are a believer, then Christ has already borne the punishment of their sin on the cross. You have no right to exact double payment. Forgiveness is not optional. It's an expression of faith in the sufficiency of Christ's atoning work.

## Forgiveness and reconciliation

Most of the forgiving we're called to do is around small things. That still matters. If we don't forgive, then these things accumulate in our minds and breed a deepening resentment or bitterness.

But what if your wife has an affair or you catch your husband viewing pornography or your husband is violent towards you?

Reconciliation involves repentance. Without repentance there can't be true reconciliation. God is not reconciled to us without our repentance (thankfully He graciously gives us repentant hearts through the work of the Holy Spirit).

Love doesn't mean we should be reconciled to someone who is unrepentant. And even when there is repentance, trust will take time to be restored. Trust is not something we're obliged to feel. We're not called to trust someone who is untrustworthy. Forgiveness is not earned and making people earn forgiveness is not true forgiveness. But trust does have to be earned.

If someone is unrepentant, then we might not trust them and might not be reconciled to them. But we should continue to love the person. That can be very tough, but we are called to love. Our example is God, who sends rain on the righteous and unrighteous and loved us even when we were His enemies. A good test of whether we love those who have wronged us is how we pray for them. And love means a willingness to forgive if and when they repent.

## Questions for reflection

- ❓ How do you typically respond when you're wronged by your partner?
- ❓ How does your attitude to your partner compare with God's attitude to you?
- ❓ Can you think of examples (hypothetical or real) in which someone might demand that forgiveness must be earned or trust must be given?

## Ideas for action

Here are some practical tips for resolving disagreements:

### 🔽 Repent rather than dissect
Most arguments involve culpability on both sides. So if you can, go straight to repentance and asking forgiveness without a forensic dissection of guilt. However guilt should be apportioned, you've probably sinned far more than you realize.

### 🔽 Forget if you can, talk it through if you must
If you can just forget an offense against you, then do so. If it continues to annoy you or you brood on it, then raise it as an issue to talk through.

### Cool off

It may not always be best to talk about something in the heat of the moment. But do so before the sun goes down.

### Use "I" statements rather than "you" statements

"You" statements pass judgment and put people on the defensive ("You don't help around the house." "You were horrible to me."). "I feel" statements are less inflammatory and open the way to discussion and problem solving. Ban the words "always" and "never" from arguments.

### Listen carefully and then repeat it back to ensure you understand

Get rid of distractions (TV turned off, children out of the way). Sit close to each other. Hold hands. Look at each other. Don't interrupt one another. One of you may find it helpful to write something down to help articulate your feelings. Above all, try to understand how each other feels. Try to repeat what the other person is saying and feeling until the other person is happy that you understand properly.

### Ask for forgiveness

Don't say: "I'm sorry". That requires no response. Ask: "Will you forgive me?"

### Move on

Love keeps no record of wrongs. Don't hold grudges. Make up after an argument in some constructive way. Do something positive together.

**part three**

# gospel-centered sex

# 11 Enjoying sex

It's our duty to enjoy marital sex.

## Consider this

Dirty jokes. Lewd comments. Suggestive remarks. Wolf whistles. Men trying to look down her blouse or feel her bottom. "Men seem obsessed by sex," Penny thought. It was horrible. She felt demeaned by it all. Threatened. Vulnerable. It all seemed so predatory.

And now Phil seemed just as bad. She didn't really know what she expected from her new husband. But it certainly wasn't this. Sex was okay, though she never really looked forward to it. But Phil seemed to want it every night. Sometimes he would grope her in the kitchen or wink suggestively when he talked about going to bed.

"Is this normal?" Penny asked Maria, blushing slightly.

"I wish," thought Maria.

## Biblical background

*Read the description of the lovers' wedding and wedding night in Song of Songs 4 v 12 – 5 v 1*

- ❓ What does 4 v 12 describe?
- ❓ What do verses 13-15 describe?
- ❓ What does 4 v 16 mean (compare it with 2 v 7 and 3 v 5)?
- ❓ What does 5 v 1 describe?
- ❓ What view of sex does this passage reflect?

**Read all about it**

### Sex is God's good creation

In chapter 4 of *The Song of Songs*, following the wedding of the young man and woman in chapter 3, we enter the honeymoon suite. We get a detailed, passionate, intimate celebration of her body. Finally the husband enters her "garden", sheltered in her thighs, a place no one has entered before. He gathers her myrrh, eats her honey, drinks her wine. There are 111 lines before this verse and 111 lines after it. This is the climax—in every way! This Song of Songs, the epitome of wisdom, has at its heart a celebration of sexual intercourse.

Sex is God's idea. Nothing constrained God's creation. He wasn't making the best of bad materials. He could have made it any way He liked and He made it with sex. Sex is good and it's to be received with thanksgiving. To think sex is dirty or bad is to impugn God's goodness (1 Timothy 4 v 1-5). Sex is too precious to be "put up" with. It seems God made the clitoris for no other purpose than for women to enjoy sex!

In our culture sex is everywhere. It's used to sell adverts. We gossip about the sex lives of celebrities. Porn is readily available. Yet along the way, sex has been emptied of its meaning. It's mystery and power have been stolen by this endless exhibitionism. Never before has sex offered so much and given so little. Our sexuality is supposed to be like Niagara Falls, constrained by the rocks into a powerful, surging rush. But our culture has made sexuality more like the Mississippi Delta: unconstrained, it has spread out wide and thin and muddy. The Bible gives us safeguards not to stop us being spoiled by sex, but to stop sex being spoiled by us.

### Sex is an act of unification

Sex is not simply a pleasurable activity. It creates a new reality. Sex unites two people into one flesh (Genesis 2 v 23-24). Sex is designed by God to complete or fulfil or bind together the companionship of marriage. So sex is very powerful. It binds together at the deepest of levels. Quoting Genesis 2, Jesus says: "'For this reason a man will leave his father and mother and be united to his wife, and the two will become one flesh.' So they are no longer two, but one. Therefore what God has joined together, let man not separate" (Mark 10 v 7-9). Who unites people through sex? Not merely the man and woman involved, but God Himself.

So sex is not just about satisfying physical urges or getting physical pleasure. It unites me to another person. This means sex outside of marriage is a sham, binding together what is not together. You can no more "try out" sex or marriage than you can try out birth. The very act produces a new reality that cannot be undone.

## Sex is an act of disclosure

"Knowing" in the Bible is a metaphor for sex not because the writers were coy, but because sex really is about knowing. When you remove your clothes, you're opening up your life. The removal of clothes and the offer of physical intimacy are powerful markers of self-giving. We're offering the other person, not only a view of our bodies, but also a view of our souls.

Before the fall into sin, "the man and his wife were both naked, and they felt no shame" (Genesis 2 v 25). But after their sin they feel their nakedness because now they have something to hide (Genesis 3 v 7). Covering their bodies is a sign that sin has shamed their hearts. They also felt vulnerable to one another. One of the joys of marriage is the ability to be naked and then be embraced in your nakedness. But now they know the other is a covenant-breaker who cannot be trusted, who might exploit their nakedness with jokes, scorn, assault, or defilement.

The good news is that God covers our shame. In Genesis 3 v 21 God provides "garments of skin" for Adam and Eve. An animal is sacrificed so that their shame might be covered. It's a pointer to the righteousness of Christ, who clothes God's people through His sacrificial death.

Meanwhile, sex flourishes in the context of covenant commitment. I really believe that couples committed to the covenant of marriage have the best sex. They have years to get to know one another sexually. They have a commitment to resolving conflict. They have a commitment to self-giving.

## Be committed to sex

Don't be indifferent to sex. Some people in the Corinthian church were downplaying the importance of sex (1 Corinthians 7 v 1-5). But viewing sex as bad, Paul suggests, will lead to dangerous temptations. Then he says a husband should "fulfil his marital duty to his wife" and *vice versa*. You owe it to one another to satisfy each other's sexual desires. When you married, you gave up your rights over your body. You entrusted them into the hands of your husband or wife.

Choosing sexual *in*activity within marriage is just as wrong as choosing sexual activity outside marriage. If you're not in the mood, then still be available for sex. If you *are* in the mood, then try to set the mood for your spouse by making them feel cherished.

**Questions for reflection**

- Do you have a negative view of sex, perhaps thinking it's not really godly behavior?
- Where do you think this comes from?
- How does the gospel renew your view of sex?
- Think about sexual turn-offs: exhaustion, criticism, bad breath, body odor, no foreplay, in-laws in the next room, being treated like a servant rather than a friend.
  - Which of these are factors in your marriage? Are there other turn-offs for you?
  - Which of these can you do something about?
  - Which can you plan round?
  - Which will you have to be patient with?

## Ideas for action

- ▽ **Don't let children become the center of your marriage.** That's good for them because it teaches them that they're not the center of the world.
- ▽ **Understand the times.** Young children especially can provide the emotional intimacy that mothers previously looked for in marriage, and also the hormone that enables breast-feeding reduces libido. Husbands need to appreciate this and be patient, while wives need to appreciate their husband's needs.
- ▽ **Don't make spontaneity the measure of good sex.** Parents of young children are too exhausted to feel spontaneous about sex. Plan to get the children to bed early; create time to relax. You might want to make your bedroom a private space from which the children are normally excluded. Or leave the children with the grandparents while you get away for the weekend.

# 12 Loving sex

**Principle**

Good sex begins long before you take your clothes off.

 **Consider this**

It was so nice to sink into bed.

What a day! Megan's boss was under pressure from her superiors and seemed to be passing all the pressure on to the team. Everyone had been on edge and her colleague, Sally, had been weepy again in the afternoon.

In her lunch break she'd managed to do the shopping, but that meant she'd had to eat lunch at her desk. The train was late and then when she finally got home, she'd walked in the door to the sound of her teenage sons in the middle of a raging argument.

Once she'd sorted that one out (sort of), she started on the dinner. Sam and the boys wolfed it down as usual. "How was your day?" she'd asked him. "Okay. Usual stuff. I've got a meeting at church this evening." And so she was left to tidy the house and get the boys to bed again. After that it was ironing.

It was so nice to sink into the soft bed.

Then she felt Sam's cold hand reaching under her nightie. "Oh no," she thought. "Not tonight."

## Biblical background

*Read Song of Songs 4 v 1-16*

- ❓ What does all the imagery used in this passage represent?
- ❓ How might you express the same ideas using contemporary imagery?
- ❓ How do you think the Beloved felt as her Lover said this?
- ❓ What does she say in response (verse 16)?

## Read all about it

Marriage and sexuality are designed to reveal the passionate love of God for His people. This means *good sex* is sex within marriage that enables us to know God in Christ more fully. It's sex that reflects the relationship of God in Christ to His people.

So good sex is intimate, affectionate, gentle, sacrificial, personal and pleasurable. Just as God deals with us gently, so we should be gentle with our partners. Just as God in Christ sacrifices His life for His people, so we should put the pleasure of our partner before our own pleasure in intercourse. It means that masochistic sex, sado-masochistic sex, aggressive sex talk and sex involving some form of domination or enacted domination, even when these involve mutual consent, *must be* regarded as bad sex. Because they don't model Christ's sacrificial love for His people.

Sex teaches us the pleasure of giving of *myself to my partner*: the pleasure of giving pleasure; the love of loving; the honor of honoring; the blessing of being a blessing.

This also means that sex doesn't begin when you remove your clothes. If serving your partner is what matters most, then you'll make love throughout the day, through little acts and words of service, kindness and affection. Making love is not synonymous with intercourse, but expresses a lifestyle of service and affection. Sex can begin with doing the dishes—an act that shows your spouse that you cherish them.

Emotional intimacy and disclosure come before physical intimacy and nakedness. In this sense, we make love all day. Every communication communicates not only information, but also how you feel about your spouse and how you value them.

The word "intercourse" is used in two senses: sexual activity and conversation. Both these senses of the word belong together. Conversation is the beginning of foreplay. The Song of Songs is full of words of mutual admiration. Tell your spouse what it is that you love about them. Not just *that* you love them, but *why*. What is it that you admire about them?

The Lover in the *Song of Songs* woos his Beloved with his words. It's a generalization, but women are often turned on by what they feel and what they hear, rather than by what they see. C. J. Mahaney says: "Before you touch her body, touch her heart and mind".[1] And his wife, Carolyn, says: "The sexiest organ of the human body lies between our ears".[2]

Men cannot roll into bed at night and expect their wife to be up for sex. She needs to be valued and treasured. You need to touch her with your words. And you need to touch her with your actions. You need to serve her. She won't feel like sex if she's tired. So cook the dinner, clean the house, bring her a drink. Make her feel that she's "my treasure, my bride" rather than "my cook, my servant". (If she feels like your servant and then you suddenly expect sex at the end of the day, she'll feel like "your servant, your prostitute".)

---

1 C. J. Mahaney, **Sex, Romance, and the Glory of God**, Multnomah, 2004, 27.

2 Carolyn Mahaney in C. J. Mahaney, **Sex, Romance, and the Glory of God,** Multnomah, 2004, 123.

So *good sex is not about quality of technique, but about quality of relationship.* Sex is not a "thing" that you do. It's inextricably embedded in a relationship. Its purpose is to celebrate and cement that relationship. The story is told of a preacher in Wales who announced a talk entitled: "How to get your wife to treat you like a king". With a title like that the men of the village packed into the hall. He stood up and simply said: "Treat her like a queen".

Sex is so equated with power and performance that it's hard for us to approach sex with humility. But humble we must be if we want to serve God and serve our spouse. Be humble enough to ask your spouse how you can be a better lover. When a three-year-old brings her father a picture, the father knows it's rubbish but thinks it's wonderful. Your wife will respond in the same way to your pathetic attempts at romance and love-making if sincerely offered!

Sex as performance is a deep and damaging undercurrent in our culture. Sex on screen is by its very nature a performance. But it's unreal, dressed up, stage managed. It's no more real than the fight sequences of an action movie or comic strip. But the real lie is not that sex is ever performed in this way, but that sex is ever a performance. There is no audience. There are simply two people expressing their love. What matters is not the gymnastics of their sexual activity nor the intensity of their orgasms, but the love they celebrate for one another.

 **Questions for reflection**

- ❓ Take it in turns to tell each other what it is that you love about each other. Not just that you love them, but why. What is it that you admire in the other?
- ❓ Do you feel most like a wife or husband, mother or father, breadwinner, counsellor, homemaker or professional?
- ❓ What do you enjoy during love-making?

# 13 Transforming sex

**Principle**

We get sex wrong because we get God wrong.

 **Consider this**

"It's so frustrating." Sam was chatting with his friend Bob. He'd wanted to talk about sex with someone for ages, but hadn't quite had the courage. But Bob's question—"How's it going with Megan?"—was as good an opening as he was ever going to get.

"I want sex more often than Megan does. I don't know what I'm doing wrong. I try to romance her during the evening, but she just gives me an I-know-where-this-is-leading look. Then at bedtime I say: "How about it?" and she says: "If we must". If we must! You can guess how that makes me feel."

"But she's willing to have sex with you?" asked Bob.

"Yes, sort of. But only out of pity. I don't want sex out of pity. I want her to want it. I want to give her pleasure."

Bob started to respond. But Sam was in full flow by now.

"And another thing. We kind of always arrange it. Why can't we just be overcome with passion? Maybe not all the time, but sometimes."

Bob paused, checking that Sam had stopped.

**Biblical background**

*Read Romans 1 v 18-25*

? Why does sex go wrong?

? How can exchanging the truth of God for a lie lead to problems with sex?

? How can worshiping created things rather than the Creator lead to problems with sex?

 **Read all about it**

That which most threatens our relationship with God—our idolatrous desires—is that which most threatens good sex. Consider how idolatrous desires can corrupt sex within marriage.

## When you don't get enough sex...

It's all too common to find in marriages a tension between husband and wife over how often they have sex, usually with the husband wanting sex more than their wife is able or willing to give.

Over time this can have a corrosive effect. The husband feels frustrated and blames the wife. The wife feels under pressure and that's not a good context in which to enjoy sex. Her desire diminishes still further and the husband becomes more frustrated. The marriage can enter a vicious cycle of pressure and frustration. Sex mattering more than the person with whom we're having sex is a sure sign that sex has become an idol. Our allegiance to sex has become greater than our allegiance to God.

The cycle is broken by a determination to put your partner's desires above your own. It might mean saying: "I don't really feel like sex tonight, but I don't mind if you're keen". It might mean saying: "Thank you, but we're both a bit tired. How about we have an early night tomorrow and just have a quick cuddle tonight."

## Making love without making love

Any sex in which we objectify our partner is bad sex. We objectify our partner when we consider them a means by which we can gain sexual pleasure, rather than a person with whom we have a relationship. Again, sex itself has become more important than honoring God by serving our partner. So don't love sex more than you love your spouse. Don't view sex as something in its own right. Otherwise your spouse will become merely the "thing" which gives you sex. See sex always and only as the flowering of the love you have together.

Objectifying our partner can occur if we put our pleasure above theirs. It can also occur if, through fantasy, we transpose ourselves into another situation or imagine having sex with another person. When this occurs, we are committing adultery even as we have sex with our spouse.

The same can be said about wearing special clothing. Clothing that enhances the look of the body is entirely appropriate, and removing one another's clothing in love-making is a powerful symbol of the self-disclosure and self-offering that is taking place. But wearing provocative lingerie or other special clothing (dressing up as a nurse, for example) can be a form of objectification if it's intended to transform the person temporarily into someone else.

## When they don't seem up for it

A common complaint of husbands is that wives are not "up for it". The complaint runs something like this. The wife is willing to have sex with the husband because she's happy to serve him and give him pleasure through sex. But she's not always interested in her own sexual pleasure. She doesn't want an orgasm every time. But this isn't enough for the husband. He wants a sexually rapacious wife. He wants her to be hungry for it.

"I only want to give her pleasure," more than one husband has told me. "What's wrong with that?" The brutal answer is that, more often than not, this is a self-deluding lie. What he in fact wants is to be *worshipped* by his wife. He wants her to acknowledge his sexual prowess and power. There may be a preoccupation with sexual performance. He wants her to come under his power, in this case his sexual power—to be helpless before him as she is overwhelmed by her desire for him, in which she worships him.

Another form this can take is the "need" for spontaneity. The husband or wife may resent planning sex or always having sex in the same context. They long for moments when they're both overcome by sexual desire. Spontaneity and variation are great. But resentment over a lack of spontaneity can be a sign that something is amiss. It may reflect a desire for moments in which your partner falls under your power and worships you.

So an obsession with "pleasuring" your spouse can in fact be self-serving. You want to be worshipped. You want to feel potent. This is idolatry. Or if you conceive of sex as a performance, then your desire is to be admired or worshipped rather than to love and be loved. This too is idolatry.

This means that serving your partner may involve allowing them the pleasure of serving you even when they don't feel up for sex. This is humbling! We don't like to think that our partners are only having sex with us because they want to serve us (out of pity, we might caricature it).

## Giving pleasure

But one of the joys of a godly marriage is that we find pleasure in giving pleasure. When our partner matters more to us than ourselves, then giving pleasure becomes itself pleasurable. You have the pleasure of knowing they have the pleasure of giving you pleasure! It creates a very different cycle to the cycle of frustration.

This reciprocal giving of pleasure and accepting of pleasure—of finding pleasure through accepting pleasure—reflects our relationship with God. In love, the pleasure of God and our pleasure cohere. God delights in our delight in Him. We delight in God's delight in us.

## Questions for reflection

? What are your sexual icons? A half-naked, young guy with a six pack? A 36-24-36 woman simpering in lingerie? An elderly couple celebrating their wedding anniversary?

? Which of these "icons" represent the truth about sex and marriage? What message does each of these "sexual icons" communicate? How do they compare with the true meaning of sex, which is to illustrate God's passionate covenant love for His people?

### Ask yourself:

? How have my idolatrous desires affected our sex life?

? Do I need to repent before God? Do I need to repent to my spouse?

? What practices strengthen or provoke my idolatrous desires? How can we change these?

# **14** Gospel-centered beauty

**Principle**

Love finds us beautiful and love makes us beautiful.

 **Consider this**

"You look gorgeous," Wayne said. Who was he kidding? She saw the pictures in the magazines. Her waist was too fat, her breasts too large, her hair too flat. No, she wasn't beautiful. Maybe she should go on a diet. Again.

Leona had borne Devon two lovely children. But now she'd put on weight and there were wrinkles around her eyes. Once he'd thought she was stunning, but now... well, now it was hard not to eye up the girls in the office.

"You're so beautiful," Fred said, taking hold of Elsie's hand.

"I'm 72 years old," she exclaimed with a laugh.

"And still as beautiful as the day I married you."

"I hardly think so."

"It's your eyes. When you smile at me with love, the rest of the world disappears."

"You soppy old thing," she said, smiling to herself as she gave him a gentle push.

**Biblical background**

*Read 1 Peter 3 v 3-6*

**?** Complete this table to contrast the types of beauty described.

|  | outward beauty | inward beauty |
|---|---|---|
| How long will it last? | *fading* |  |
| What is its value? | *expensive* |  |
| Whose attention are you trying to attract? | *men* |  |
| What is your preoccupation? | *self* |  |
| Who are your models? | *the latest film stars and fashion models* |  |

**?** How do we achieve inward beauty?

 **Read all about it**

Our culture holds out a standard of beauty that is literally unattainable. The images that feed this vision of beauty are fake, created by computer software. There has to be a gap between you and the image so that you buy the products being sold, in a futile attempt to measure up.

We live with a definition of beauty that no one can attain, and then we are invited to rank one another by this unattainable standard. No wonder so many people feel dissatisfied with their appearance. Our partner cannot possibly hope to measure up to the expectation created in the media—especially as they grow older.

Not only is our ideal of beauty unattainable, it's also artificial. In our culture being tanned is considered beautiful. But in Solomon's times white skin was highly prized. The young woman in the *Song* says: "I am dark but beautiful ... Don't stare at me because I am dark" (1 v 5-6, NLT). It's about wealth. Back then, dark skin meant you were a peasant working long hours outside. Today dark skin means you can afford foreign holidays or can lounge in the sun. It's the same with body size. Westerners value thin women; Africans fat women. The point is that our idea of beauty is shaped by the culture around us plus commercial interests.

Imagine a world in which a young man never sees half-naked, provocative women. On his wedding night his bride comes to him and he thinks her the most exquisite being on the planet. Sadly this is not our world. But as Christians, as wives, as husbands, we are to be counter-cultural in this area. "Do not conform any longer to the pattern of this world,"—to this world's ideas of beauty—"but be transformed by the renewing of your mind. Then you will be able to test and approve what God's will is—his good, pleasing and perfect will" (Romans 12 v 2).

## Choose to find your spouse beautiful

Don't think the catwalk and the billboard define beauty and then assess your spouse by that standard. Who says a flat stomach is the epitome of beauty? Why can't you find curves attractive? Who says wrinkles are ugly?

"Rejoice in the wife of your youth. She is a loving deer, a graceful doe. Let her breasts satisfy you always. May you always be capti-vated by her love" (Proverbs 5 v 18-19, NLT). The truth is that it's a choice; it's a command; it's wisdom to find your wife beautiful. To enjoy her breasts—and not to wish they were bigger, smaller, younger, someone else's. And it's not a hard command—it is, after all, a command to fondle your wife's breasts! It commands enjoy-ment—to enjoy your wife.

## Choose to be beautiful in the eyes of your spouse

Accept that you are beautiful in the eyes of your spouse rather than measuring yourself against the false images of magazines and adverts. "But, he's biased," you might say. But so are the advertisers! They want people to feel ugly so people purchase their products. Your spouse's "bias" is love.

At the beginning of the Song of Songs the young woman is self-conscious. "Don't stare at me because I am dark" (1 v 5-6, NLT). At the end she puffs out her breasts to her lover and says: "I was a virgin, like a wall; now my breasts are like towers. When my lover looks at me, he is delighted with what he sees" (8 v 10, NLT). His delight makes her beautiful. If your husband (or wife) says you're beautiful, then you *are* beautiful in the eyes of everyone who matters.

I believe people look their most beautiful when they smile. So when people look in the mirror with self-critical eyes, they don't see beauty and so they think they're not beautiful. But my wife is *so* beautiful when she smiles at me with love.

## Value inward beauty above outward beauty

We need to value inner beauty over outward beauty, both in what we cultivate for ourselves and what we look for in others.

Pursuing outward beauty is not inherently wrong. God is the Creator, making a beautiful world and delighting in creativity. God is not forbidding outward beauty.

1 Peter 3 v 3 literally says: "Your beauty should not come from outward adornment, such as braided hair and the wearing of gold jewelry *and clothes*" (it doesn't say "fine clothes"). Peter is not forbidding wearing clothes and nor is he forbidding braiding your hair or wearing jewelry. He is forbidding a preoccupation with such things. We should not look to looks for acceptance through outward beauty. The alternative is not no clothing! The alternative is the pursuit of inward beauty. True beauty is:

- inward rather than outward
- precious rather than expensive
- unfading rather than fading

True beauty consists of "a gentle and quiet spirit". This doesn't mean timid. In fact women are not to give in to fear (verse 6). The word "master" doesn't mean Sarah was Abraham's slave (it's a different Greek word to the one translated "master" in 2 v 18). It means she addressed him with respect, honor and submission. Indeed, Jesus described Himself as "gentle" (Matthew 11 v 29), and all Christians are told to live "a quiet life" (1 Thessalonians 4 v 11).

1 Peter 3 v 5 explains what a gentle and quiet spirit involves:

| gentle | quiet |
|---|---|
| = not assertive, pushy or demanding your own way | = without agitated emotions like worry, bitterness, anger |
| the fruit of putting others first | the fruit of trusting God |
| the holy women of old made themselves beautiful by submitting to their husbands | the holy women of old made themselves beautiful by trusting God |

And here's the lovely thing: if you attract someone with your inner beauty, then they'll always be attracted to you. You can maintain inner beauty. But outward beauty is always fading. And if your relationship is based on outward beauty alone, then it will inevitably fail as time takes its toll on your body.

**Questions for reflection**

▢ What outward features do you find beautiful in your spouse?

▢ What inward features do you find beautiful in your spouse?

▢ What could your spouse do to make you feel more treasured?

▢ Do you struggle to believe your spouse when they say you're beautiful? Why is this? What standard of beauty are you using?

▢ Think of a creative way to express your appreciation of your spouse.

# 15 Conclusion: Marriage is not forever

Find your identity and joy in God rather than in marriage.

 **Consider this**

Chuck and Chloe sat snuggled up on the sofa together, looking into each other's eyes. They were so absorbed in one another, Isaac noticed. They seemed oblivious to everyone else at the party. They were in their own perfect, private world. "He's all I've ever hoped for," Chloe had told him the other day. "He makes me feel complete." "I'm so looking forward to being married," Chuck had said. "It's what I've always wanted."

Eight months later they were sat on the sofa in Isaac's office. Holding hands, but not quite so close together.

"Our marriage is not quite what we expected it would be," said Chuck in his usual measured way.

"He used to be so attentive," cut in Chloe. "But now we're married he's always working or going out with his mates."

*"Not always!"*

"Yes, and we're always arguing about things. Not big things— we're not about to split up or anything. But we seem to get on each other's nerves. And another thing. I was so looking forward to being Mrs Williams, but now I'm not really sure what my role is. Chuck's so used to looking after himself that I'm not sure what I'm supposed to do. I feel like a spare part."

"I never thought we'd have problems in our marriage, certainly not so soon as this," said Chuck.

Isaac smiled as he wondered where to start.

**Biblical background**

*Read John 4 v 4-26*

❓ What does Jesus mean when He offers the woman "living water"? See John 7 v 37-39.

❓ Where has the woman been looking for "living water"?

❓ She tries to change the subject with a question about where we should worship. How does Jesus bring the conversation back to the key issues?

 **Read all about it**

"And they both lived happily ever after." That's how books on marriage are supposed to end. Except that marriages are not for "ever after". Some marriages end in divorce. The remainder end in death. Marriage is not forever.

With the cross at the center of your marriage and with the help of God's Spirit, you may enjoy many happy years of marriage. "For better, for worse, for richer, for poorer, in sickness and in health," people usually say in their marriage vows.

There will be good times, but there will also be bad times. You may face money worries, personal tragedies, difficult children, childlessness or disability. There will be times when you let your spouse down and times when they let you down. But by God's grace those tough times will bind you even closer together.

"For better, for worse, for richer, for poorer, in sickness and in health, 'till death do us part." Even the best marriages come to an end.

*Then the Sadducees, who say there is no resurrection, came to him with a question. "Teacher," they said, "Moses wrote for us that if a man's brother dies and leaves a wife but no children, the man must marry the widow and have children for his brother. Now there were seven brothers. The first one married and died without leaving any children. The second one married the widow, but he also died, leaving no child. It was the same with the third. In fact, none of the seven left any children. Last of all, the woman died too. At the resurrection whose wife will she be, since the seven were married to her?"*

*Jesus replied, "Are you not in error because you do not know the Scriptures or the power of God? When the dead rise, they will neither marry nor be given in marriage; they will be like the angels in heaven."* **Mark 12 v 18-25**

The Sadducees thought they had an argument that proved there was no resurrection. But, in fact, what their argument proved was that marriage is a temporary institution because there's no marriage in the new creation. Or rather *there is marriage in the new creation*, but it's the marriage of *Jesus* to His bride, *the church*. There will be no marriage in the new creation because marriage will have served its great purpose: to point to the relationship of God to His people. The illustration will give way to the reality.

*And I heard a loud voice from the throne saying, "Now the dwelling of God is with men, and he will live with them. They will be his people, and God himself will be with them and be their God. He will wipe every tear from their eyes. There will be no more death or mourning or crying or pain, for the old order of things has passed away."* **Revelation 21 v 3-4**

Marriage is really important because it points to God's relationship with His people. And yet marriage is *not really, really* important—it's not the ultimate thing in life—for the same reason, because it points beyond itself to God's relationship with His people.

Because it illustrates God and His people, we need to work at marriage, protect marriage, and stick with marriage. Our marriages need to show the same passionate love and covenant loyalty that God shows. But because that illustration will one day give way to reality, marriage is not the most important thing in our lives. God is ultimate, not our spouse, nor our marriage, nor sex. God is the one who truly completes us. God is the one who truly loves us. God is the one who will always stick by us. God is the one who truly satisfies us and God is the one who gives us identity.

## This is so important

You may be approaching marriage. And maybe you think this will be it. Your spouse will make you happy ever after. Being married will complete you. Maybe you've lived for the moment when you walk down the aisle dressed up like a mering!

You're going to be in for a rude awakening. You were made to know God, to be satisfied in Him, to find identity in Him. If you think a mere man or woman or marriage itself can do this, then you're setting up massively unrealistic expectations. And that's not fair on your spouse. You're setting them up to disappoint you.

Don't go into marriage thinking it will provide for you what only God can provide. Only as you find contentment and identity in God will you be free truly to enjoy your spouse.

Time and again I've found that the couples who were most absorbed with one another during their engagement had the rockiest first year of marriage. They thought the other was all they needed in life. But your spouse turns out to be just another sinful human being with bad breath and annoying habits.

Or maybe you're in the middle of marriage and it's not all you hoped it would be. You've discovered your spouse can be annoying, boring, frustrating, frustrated. Maybe they have been hit by illness. Maybe the rigors of childcare have taken the zest out of your love life. Maybe you're arguing because money is tight. Marriage doesn't seem to be all it's cracked up to be. It could be that you went into marriage with unrealistic expectations, thinking it would solve your problems or fulfil your needs or satisfy your longings.

The answer is not to give up on marriage. Your marriage might just be a normal good-days-and-bad-days marriage. The answer is to find your identity in God, not in marriage. To find your joy in God, not in your spouse. Then you might become free to enjoy your spouse.

Or maybe you're the other side of marriage. Maybe divorce has left you bitter or wounded. Maybe bereavement has left you with a huge hole in your life. Marriage is not forever. It points us to the relationship of God to His people. So look to where marriage points. The pain that you feel is a reminder of God's passionate love for you. Find comfort in Him. He is the Lover who never leaves us nor forsakes us. He is the Lover who will wipe away our tears.

The Bible story ends with a marriage. God's new world is described as a wedding feast for the marriage between God's people and God's Son. "And the angel said to me, 'Write this: Blessed are those who are invited to the wedding feast of the Lamb'" (Revelation 19 v 9).

## Questions for reflection

- ❓ What are your hopes for your marriage?
- ❓ Are they things that you should be looking for from God rather than marriage?
- ❓ What are your fears for your marriage?
- ❓ Do your fears suggest you're expecting from marriage what you should look for from God?
- ❓ How can you help one another find identity and joy in God? How can you keep one another's focus on the Lord Jesus Christ?

## Ideas for action

A key way you can help one another walk with God and find joy in Christ is by reading the Bible and praying together on a regular basis. If you're not doing this already, then make a plan to start. Don't be too ambitious, especially if life is busy.

- What about reading a Bible passage each morning at breakfast?
- Or what about spending some time on Sunday evening sharing how the Holy Spirit spoke to you through the teaching at church that day, and then praying together for the coming week?
- Or what about using a book of short devotional readings plus a quick prayer when you get into bed each night?

Charles Spurgeon's classic, *The Check Book of the Bank of Faith*, would be a great book with which to start. You'll probably miss doing it two or three times a week because you're having breakfast or going to bed at different times, but that's okay because you'll still be praying together four or five times a week.

# Gospel-centered church
*becoming the community God wants you to be*

In *Gospel-centered church*, Steve Timmis and Tim Chester explain that gospel ministry is much more than simply evangelism. It is about shaping the whole of our church life and activities by the content and imperatives of the gospel. It is about ensuring that our church or group is motivated by and focused on the gospel, as opposed to our traditions. This workbook is designed to help clarify our thinking about how we should live our lives as the people of God.

# Gospel-centered life
*becoming the person God wants you to be*

How can ordinary Christians live the truly extraordinary life that God calls us to? By focusing our attention on the grace of God shown to us in the gospel, everyday problems, familiar to Christians everywhere, can be transformed as the cross of Christ becomes the motive and measure of everything we do. *Gospel-centered life* shows how every Christian can follow the way of the cross as they embrace the liberating grace of God.

# Gospel-centered family
*becoming the parents God wants you to be*

Many books aim to raise up competent, balanced parents and well-trained, well-rounded children. But Tim Chester and Ed Moll focus on families growing God-knowing, Christ-confessing, grace-receiving, servant-hearted, mission-minded believers – adults and children together. In twelve concise chapters, it takes us through the major Bible principles for family life, challenging us to become the distinctively different people that God, through His gospel, calls us to be.

# thegoodbook
## COMPANY

At The Good Book Company, we are dedicated to helping Christians and local churches grow. We believe that God's growth process always starts with hearing clearly what He has said to us through His timeless word—the Bible.

Ever since we opened our doors in 1991, we have been striving to produce resources that honor God in the way the Bible is used. We have grown to become an international provider of user-friendly resources to the Christian community, with believers of all backgrounds and denominations using our Bible studies, books, evangelistic resources, DVD-based courses and training events.

We want to equip ordinary Christians to live for Christ day by day, and churches to grow in their knowledge of God, their love for one another, and the effectiveness of their outreach.

Call us for a discussion of your needs or visit one of our local websites for more information on the resources and services we provide.

N America: www.thegoodbook.com
UK & Europe: www.thegoodbook.co.uk
Australia: www.thegoodbook.com.au
New Zealand: www.thegoodbook.co.nz

N America: 866 244 2165
UK & Europe: 0333 123 0880
Australia: (02) 6100 4211
New Zealand (+64) 3 343 1990

## www.christianityexplored.org
Our partner site is a great place for those exploring the Christian faith, with a clear explanation of the gospel, powerful testimonies and answers to difficult questions.

*One life. What's it all about?*